WOMEN COMPOSERS IN HISTORY

19 INTERMEDIATE TO LATE INTERMEDIATE PIANO PIECES BY 8 COMPOSERS

Compiled and Edited by Gail Smith

Cover Painting: *Young girl in a ball gown*, 1879 (oil on canvas), Morisot, Berthe (1841-95), Musee d'Orsay, Paris, France / Giraudon / The Bridgeman Art Library

ISBN 978-1-4768-1749-1

Visit Hal Leonard Online at
www.halleonard.com

Contact Us:
Hal Leonard
7777 West Bluemound Road
Milwaukee, WI 53213
Email: info@halleonard.com

In Europe contact:
Hal Leonard Europe Limited
Distribution Centre, Newmarket Road
Bury St Edmunds, Suffolk, IP33 3YB
Email: info@halleonardeurope.com

In Australia contact:
Hal Leonard Australia Pty. Ltd.
4 Lentara Court
Cheltenham, Victoria, 3192 Australia
Email: info@halleonard.com.au

PREFACE

The eight women composers represented in this book created their own musical identity in the history of music. Their personalities and life experiences are reflected in their music. Each was passionate about composing and performing at the piano. What makes these women stand out is the quality and originality of their work.

All eight composers were born in the nineteenth century, each highly esteemed in her own country and abroad. They were more than pianists, composers and mothers. Cécile Chaminade was an orchestra conductor. Teresa Carreño was an opera singer. Louise Farrenc compiled the most complete, comprehensive anthology of early keyboard music ever published. Her husband had been helping her when he died. Still, she continued the vast project, finishing it nine years later with twenty-three volumes. Margaret Lang was the first American woman to have her work performed by a major orchestra, her *Dramatic Overture*, Op. 12, played by the Boston Symphony in 1893. Fanny Mendelssohn composed her own wedding music the night before her betrothal; her brother had an accident and was unable to compose music as promised and have it delivered to her in time. All these women persevered despite distractions and obstacles.

The eight composers were similar in some ways. Teresa Carreño's father composed 500 exercises for his daughter and taught her to play the piano. Clara Schumann's father also composed 500 exercises for his daughter to practice. Amy Beach's mother gave her lessons when she was four years old. Fanny Mendelssohn was also four years old when her mother began her piano lessons. Margaret Lang was given piano and composition lessons from her father. Most of these women began composing at an early age. Amy Beach was just four when she composed her first song. Cécile Chaminade was eight. Teresa Carreño composed her first piece for Louis Gottschalk at the age of eight. Clara Schumann composed her opus 1 when she was just nine years old.

Clara Gottschalk lived in the shadow of her famous brother. Fanny Mendelssohn was overshadowed by her renowned brother Felix, who discouraged her from having her music published. Later he allowed six of her pieces to be published under his name. Fortunately for the music world, after Fanny married, her husband encouraged her to compose while he painted.

Terresa Carreño was a child prodigy who loved to perform. Her parents came to New York after a political revolution in Venezuela. She was invited to play the piano at the White House for Abraham Lincoln when she was just ten years old. When she was sixteen years old, she was summoned to play for Queen Victoria. Teresa Carreño was married five times, taught piano and toured as a concert artist. She composed most of her work before she married. Amy Marcy Beach's early music career was inhibited by her parents, who did not want their child prodigy to give concerts. Her parents encouraged her to marry Dr. H.H.A. Beach when she was 18. He was more than 20 years older than she. He did encourage her to compose, but she wasn't allowed to give concerts or teach piano lessons. Following the death of her husband, she was able to pursue a music career. Beach toured Europe, giving concerts with orchestras, performing her piano concerto and other works she had composed during her 25 years of marriage. (Amy Beach dedicated her piano concerto to Teresa Carreño.)

Nineteenth century women were able to combine a family and a career to a certain extent. All of these eight women were married. Clara Schumann had eight children and Teresa Carreño had five. Fanny Mendelssohn had one son. Amy Beach and Cécile Chaminade had no children. Cécile Chaminade was interviewed in October 1908 by the *New York Sun* and made these interesting comments: "Marriage must adapt itself to one's career. With a man it is all arranged and expected. If a woman is the artist it upsets the standards, usually it ruins the woman's art. Tho' I have been married and am a widow now, I feel that it is difficult to reconcile the domestic life with the artistic. A woman should choose one or the other. An artist must have freedom, not restraint, she must receive aid, not selfish, jealous exactions and complaints. When a woman of talent marries a man who appreciates that side of her, such a marriage may be ideally happy for both."

Some of these composers were piano teachers professionally. Fanny Mendelssohn taught a few children who were friends of the family. Louise Farrenc was the Professor of Piano at the Paris Conservatory for thirty years starting in 1842. Clara Schumann was an influential teacher and held the position of principal piano teacher of the Frankfurt Hochschen Conservatory from 1878–1892. Teresa Carreño taught many students, including Edward MacDowell. Margaret Lang took lessons from Edward MacDowell.

This collection includes some easier and intermediate pieces, sparkling jewels of music. As Amy Beach said, "The monuments of a nation mark the progress of its civilization, but its intelligence and education are qualified by its music."

—Gail Smith

CONTENTS

ABOUT THE COMPOSERS

AMY MARCY BEACH
(1867–1944)

Born September 5, 1867, Henniker, New Hampshire. Her mother was her first piano teacher and realized that Amy was very sensitive to music and associated each key with a color. She composed her first piano solo when she was just four years old. When Amy was seven she played Beethoven's Sonatas, Op. 49. When she was 16, her vocal solo "A Rainy Day," with poetry by Henry Wadsworth Longfellow, was published. That same year, she performed a concerto with the Boston Symphony. Amy married Dr. H. H. A. Beach and composed a vast amount of music during their 25-year marriage. Her works include the *Gaelic Symphony*, the Piano Concerto in C-sharp minor, the opera *Cabildo*, numerous piano solos and over 150 vocal solos. In 1892 she became the first female composer to have a piece perfomed by the New York Symphony society. Beach died in New York City on December 27, 1944.

TERESA CARREÑO
(1853–1917)

Born December 22, 1853, Caracas, Venezuela. Her father taught her piano and composed 500 exercises for her to play in rotation every three days. The family fled Venezuela during the revolution of 1862 and arrived in New York. Teresa was a child prodigy and gave concerts throughout America and even played at the White House for President Abraham Lincoln. She took lessons from the famous pianist Louis Gottschalk, for whom she composed her first piece at the age of eight. Carreño became a famous composer and concert pianist, whose career spanned 55 years. She died in New York City on June 12, 1917. A postage stamp in her honor was issued in Venezuela in 1938.

CÉCILE CHAMINADE
(1857–1944)

Born August 8, 1857, Paris. Both her parents were musical. Her father played the violin and her mother played the piano, giving her daughter lessons for many years. Georges Bizet, a neighbor, recognized Cécile's talent after seeing a piece she had composed at the age of eight. In 1877, Chaminade began her professional concert debuts and soon began performing her own works. She was the first woman to make a living as a composer. Her most famous piano solo was "Scarf Dance," which sold millions of copies during her lifetime. She was also a conductor and held a government appointment at the Office of Public Instruction in France. Chaminade died in Monte Carlo on April 13, 1944.

LOUISE DUMONT FARRENC
(1804–1875)

Born May 31, 1804, Paris. She was a prolific composer and professor of piano at the Paris Conservatory for over thirty years. Louise married a scholar with whom she compiled the twenty-three volume *Le trésor des pianists* described as the most complete collection of keyboard music ever compiled. Of her 51 numbered works, 32 are for solo piano, including four books of etudes. Farrenc died in Paris on September 15, 1875.

FANNY MENDELSSOHN HENSEL
(1805–1847)

Born November 14, 1805, Hamburg, Germany. A prodigy who grew up in a wealthy family, Fanny's mother began teaching her piano along with her younger brother Felix. By the time she was 13, Fanny could play Bach's entire *Well-Tempered Clavier* from memory. Felix and Fanny both composed at a young age. She was just as talented as her brother, but was told by her father that she must not have music as her career and was not to perform in public. Her brother published several of her pieces under his name and became the famous one in the family. Fanny married an artist who encouraged her to compose while he painted. Fanny and Felix were always very close and each admired the other's work. The Mendelssohns had regular Sunday concerts at their estate with famous guests such as Robert and Clara Schumann in attendance. Fanny died in the family auditorium on May 17, 1847 while rehearsing with a choir for the upcoming Sunday concert. (Felix died six months later.)

MARGARET RUTHVEN LANG
(1867–1972)

Born November 27, 1867, Boston. Her father, Benjamin Lang, taught her piano and composition. She later studied with Edward MacDowell. Lang composed her *Dramatic Overture*, Op. 12 in 1893 which was performed by the Boston Symphony Orchestra, making her the first woman in the United States to have a work performed by a major orchestra. Lang composed all her various works before 1930. She lived to be 104 years old, passing away on May 30, 1972 in Jamaica Plains, Massachusetts.

CLARA GOTTSCHALK PETERSON
(1837?–1910)

Born October 4, 1837, New Orleans(?). Clara was the sister of the famous pianist/composer Louis Gottschalk. Her father was Edward Gottschalk, who settled in New Orleans after arriving in America from London. Clara's father died bankrupt in 1853 and her brother assumed the father's debts, supporting his mother and sisters. Their mother died in 1856. Clara compiled her brother's diary, letters and articles after his death in 1870 and published a collection called *Notes of a Pianist*. Clara married Robert Peterson. Her compositions include many songs.

CLARA SCHUMANN
(1819–1896)

Born September 13, 1819, Leipzig, Germany. Her parents divorced when she was five. Clara's father had custody of her and began teaching her piano. Her abilities as a pianist were remarkable from an early age, touring Europe as a prodigy, admired by Chopin, Mendelssohn and Liszt. Though her father adamantly opposed the match, Clara married Robert Schumann and became a champion and famous interpreter of his works. She was a teacher, composer, concert pianist and mother of eight children. When Robert died, she supported the children and later grandchildren by composing, performing and editing music. Her compositions include orchestral and chamber pieces, many piano pieces, and numerous art songs. She died on May 20, 1896.

Secrets

from *Children's Carnival*, Op. 25, No. 5

Amy Marcy Beach
(1867–1944)

Andantino
la melodia molto tenuto

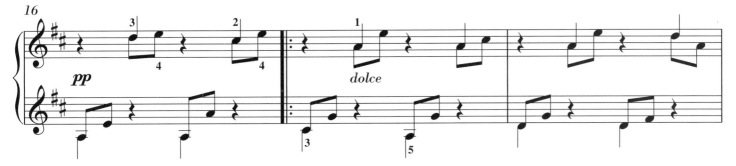

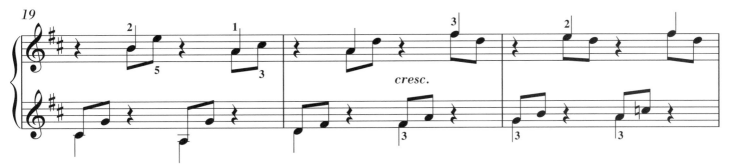

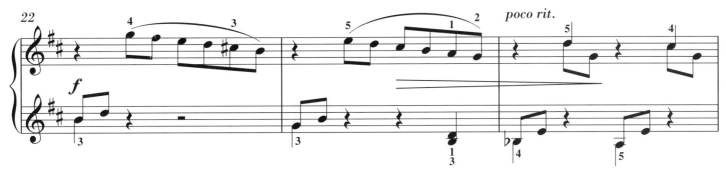

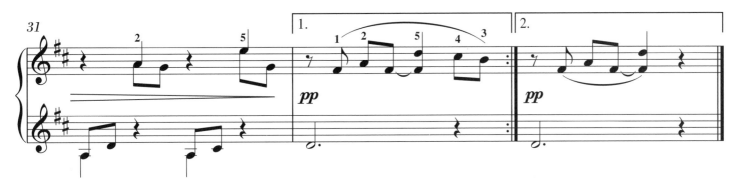

Gavotte in D minor
from *Children's Album*, Op. 36, No. 2

Amy Marcy Beach
(1867–1944)

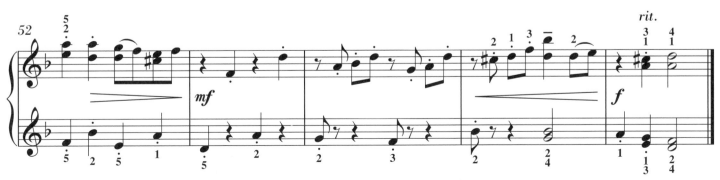

Waltz in C Major

from *Children's Album*, Op. 36, No. 3

Amy Marcy Beach
(1867–1944)

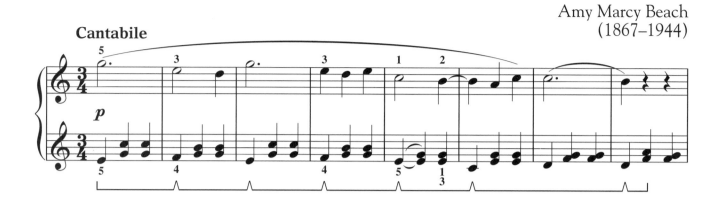

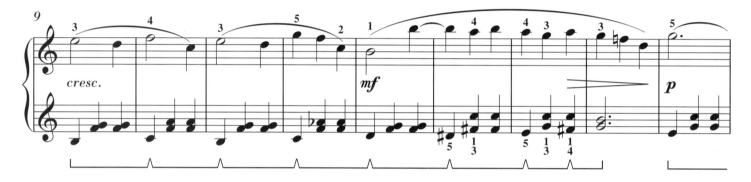

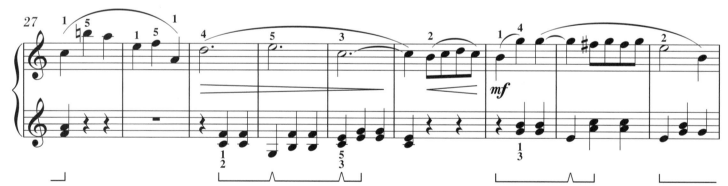

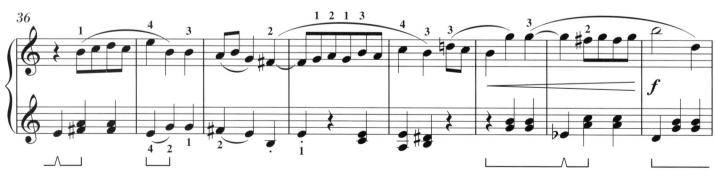

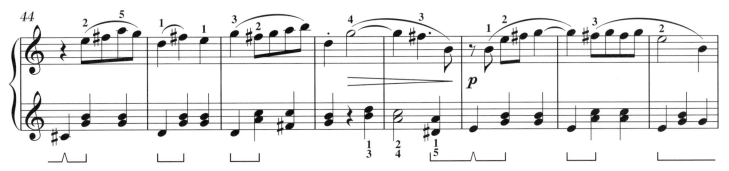

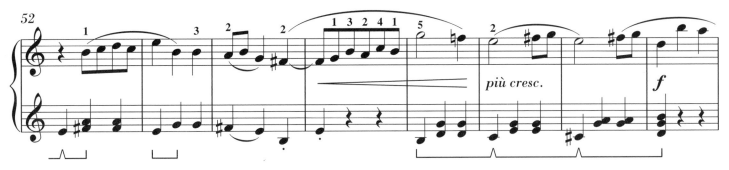

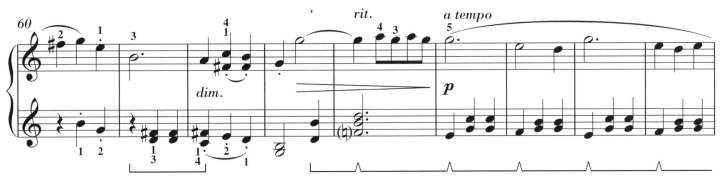

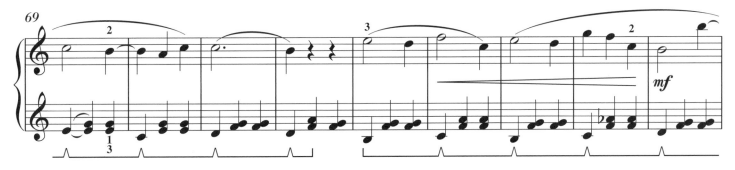

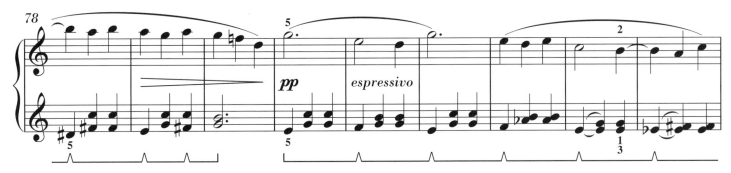

To the Junior and Juvenile Beach Clubs of Hillsboro, N.H.

Sliding on the Ice

from *From Six to Twelve*, Op. 119, No. 1

Amy Marcy Beach
(1867–1944)

Allegro vivace

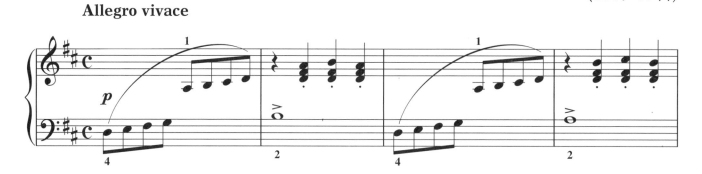

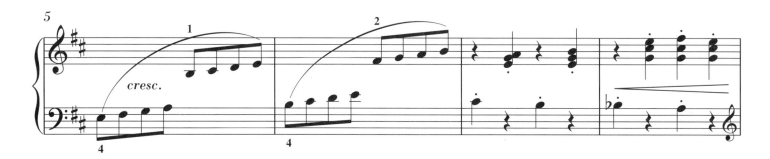

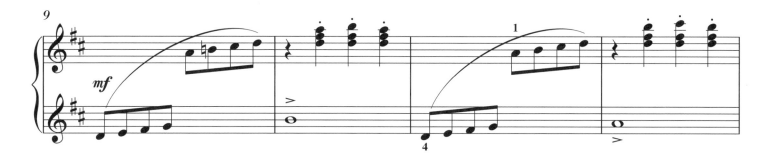

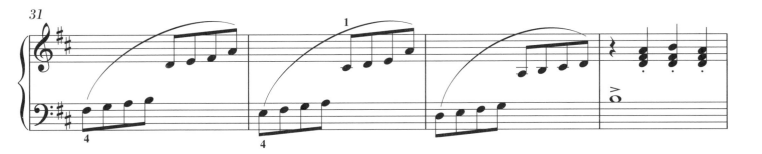

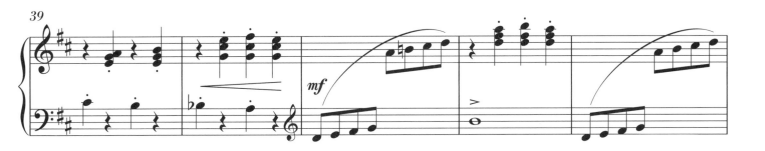

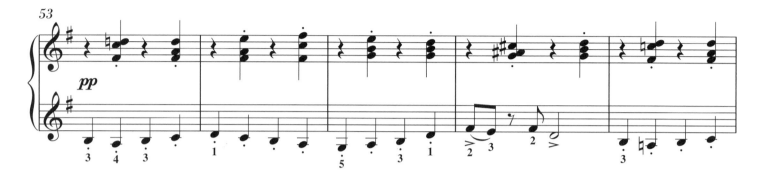

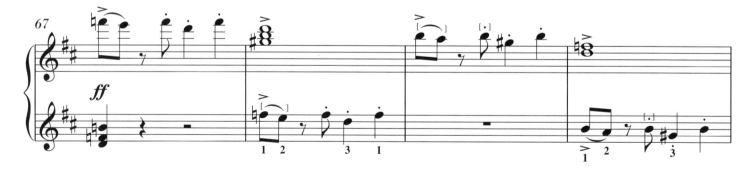

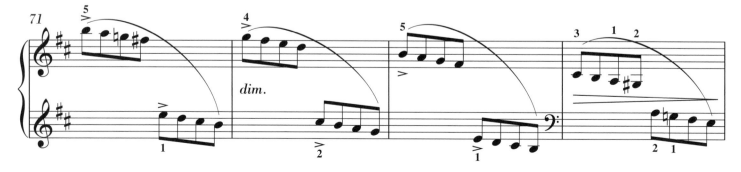

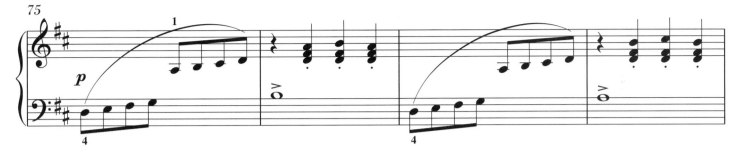

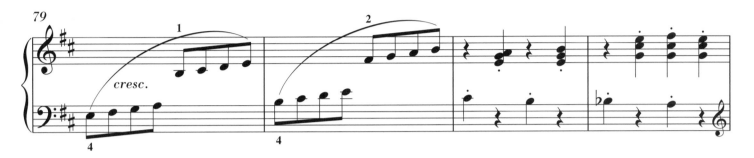

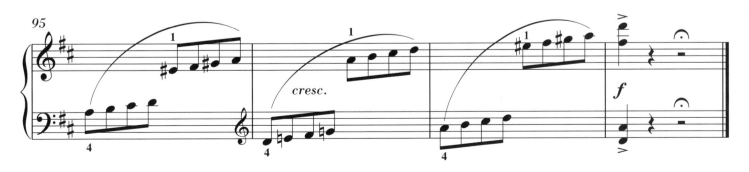

Canoeing
from *From Six to Twelve*, Op. 119, No. 3

Amy Marcy Beach
(1867–1944)

Tranquillo e sempre legato
melodia marcato

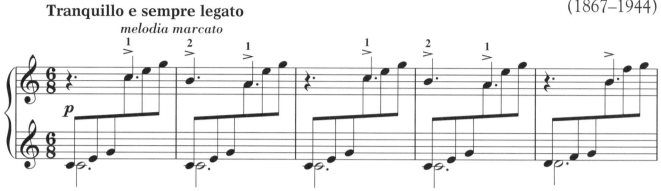

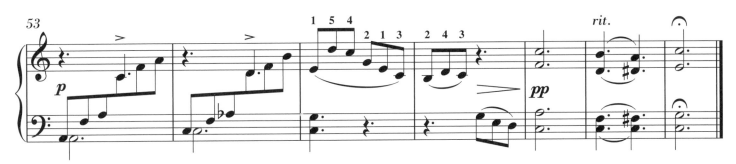

Le sommeil de l'enfant
(Berceuse), Op. 35

Teresa Carreño
(1853–1917)

Allegretto quasi andante (♩. = 48)

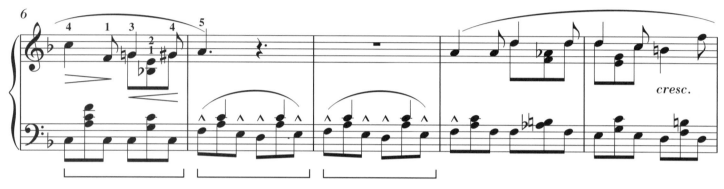

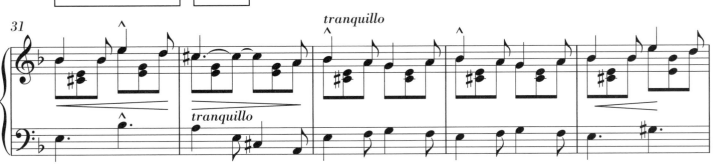

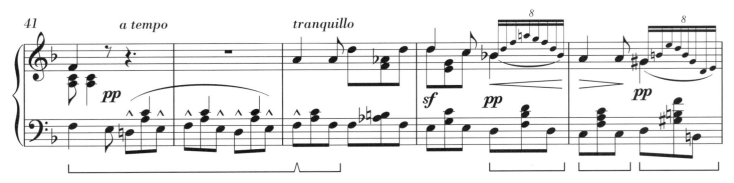

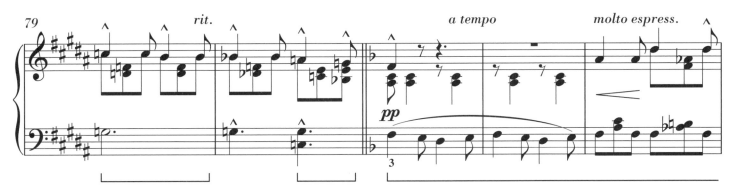

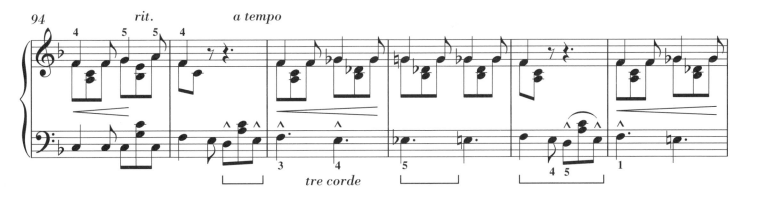

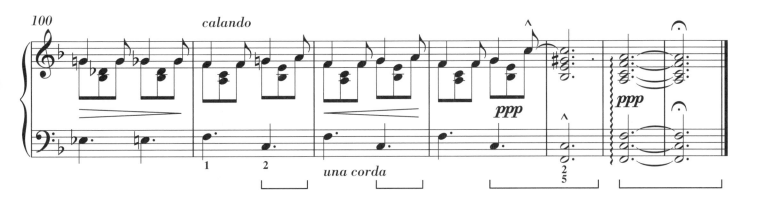

Gavotte in A minor
from *Album d'enfants*, Op. 123, No. 5

Cécile Chaminade
(1857–1944)

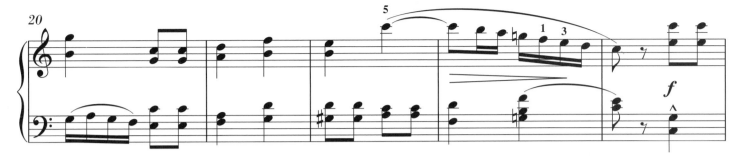

Gigue in C Major
from *Album d'enfants*, Op. 123, No. 6

Cécile Chaminade
(1857–1944)

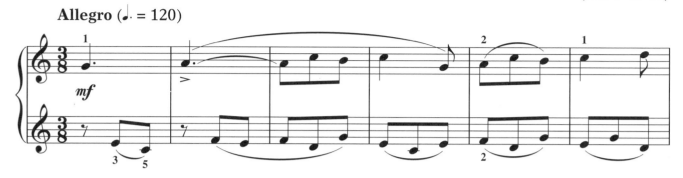

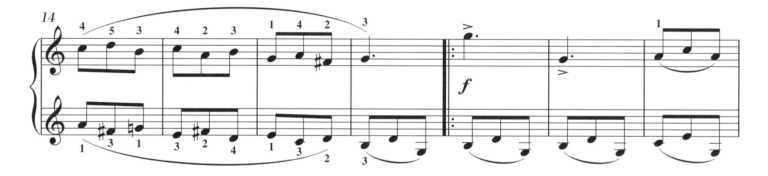

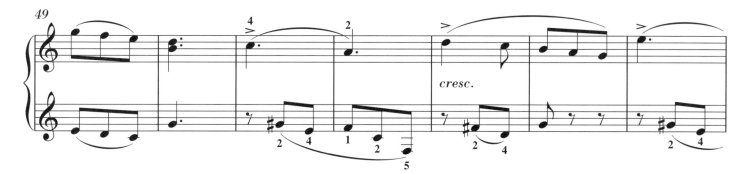

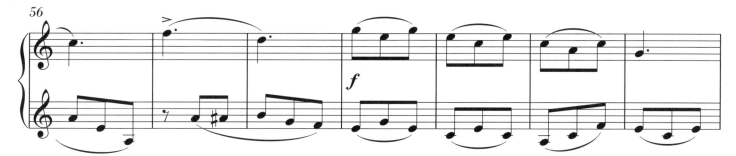

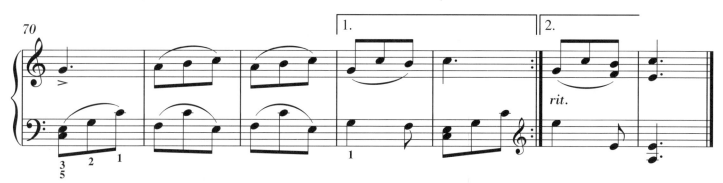

Rigaudon in A minor
from *Album d'enfants*, Op. 126, No. 3

Cécile Chaminade
(1857–1944)

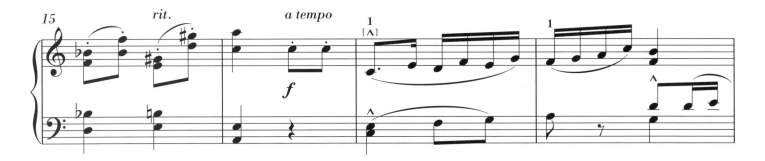

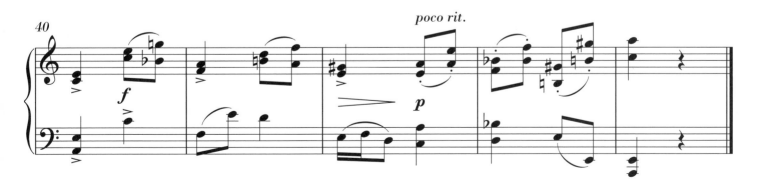

Etude in C Major

from *Vingt cinq études faciles*, Op. 50, No. 1

Louise Dumont Farrenc
(1804–1875)

Andante grazioso

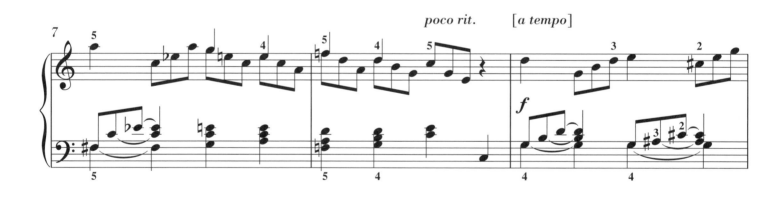

poco rit. [a tempo]

Etude in A minor

from *Vingt cinq études faciles*, Op. 50, No. 2

Louise Dumont Farrenc
(1804–1875)

Andantino (♩. = 66–80)

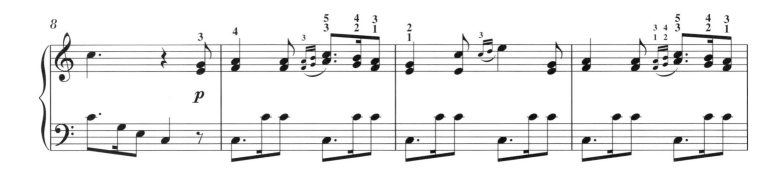

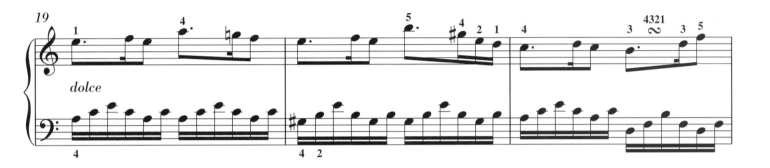

Impromptu in B minor

Louise Dumont Farrenc
(1804–1875)

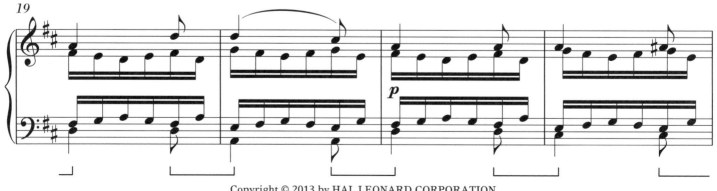

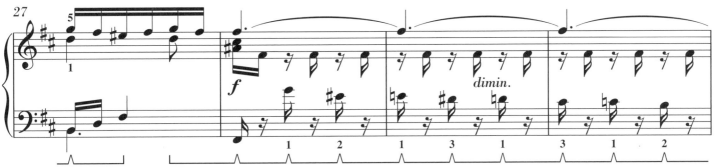

Andante con espressione

Fanny Mendelssohn Hensel
(1805–1847)

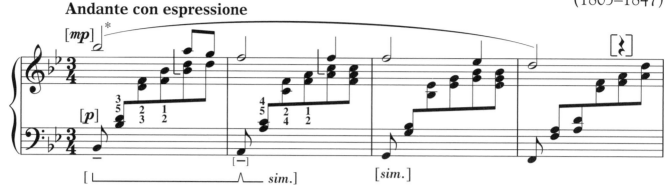

*Phrase marks are editorial suggestions.

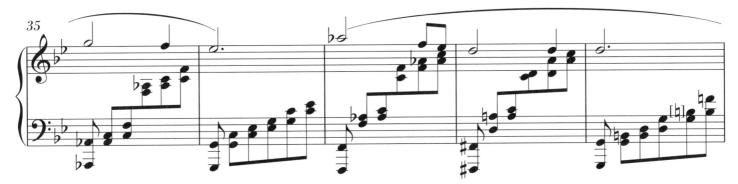

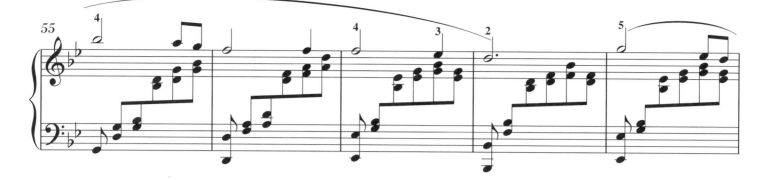

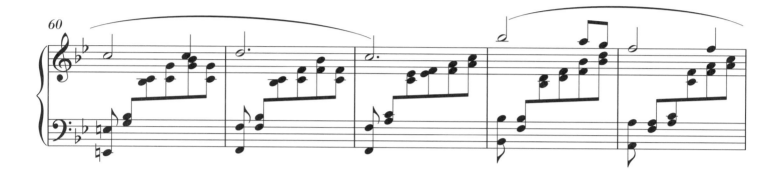

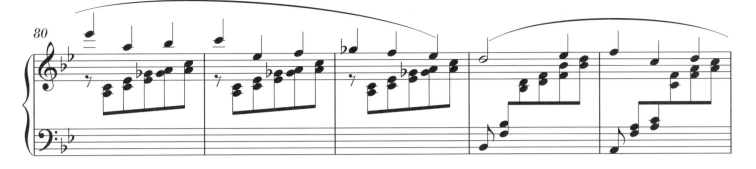

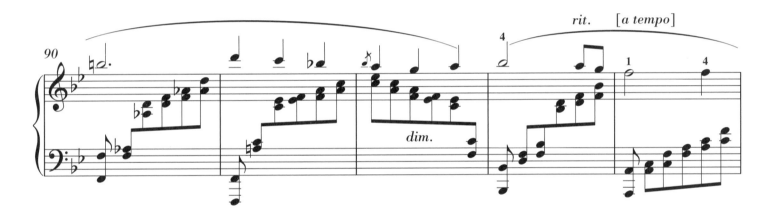

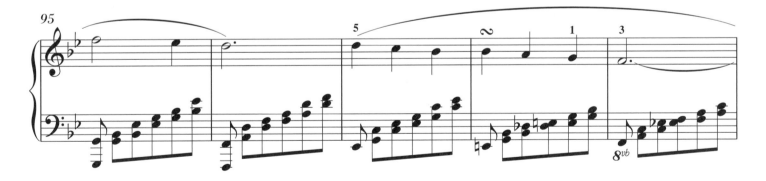

Fugue in E-flat Major

Fanny Mendelssohn Hensel
(1805–1847)

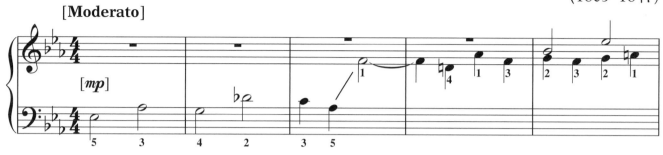

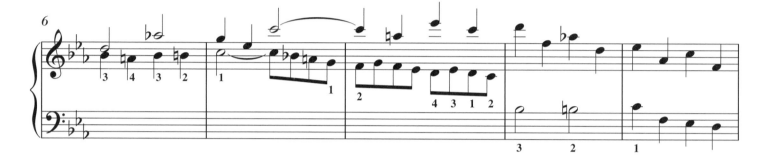

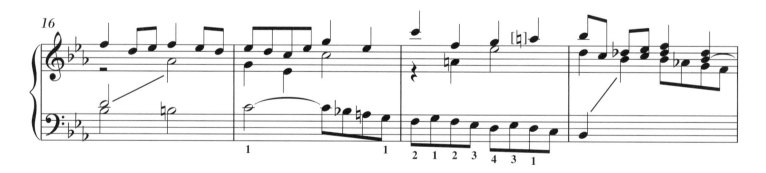

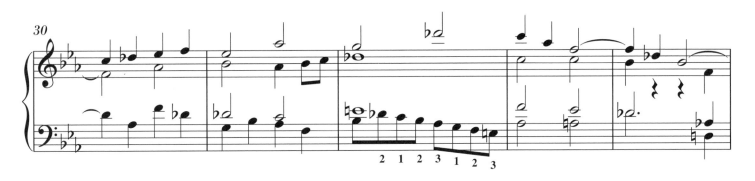

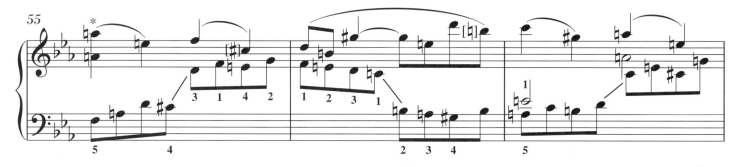

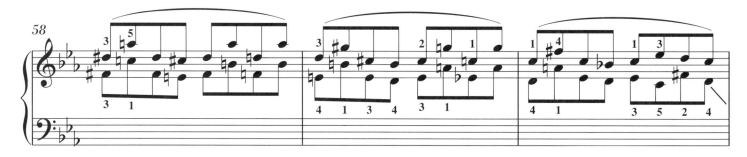

*Phrasing marks are editorial throughout.

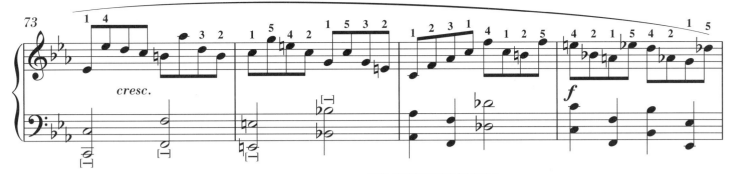

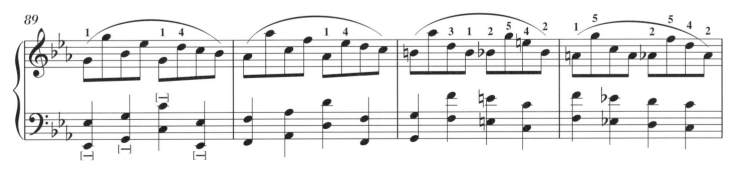

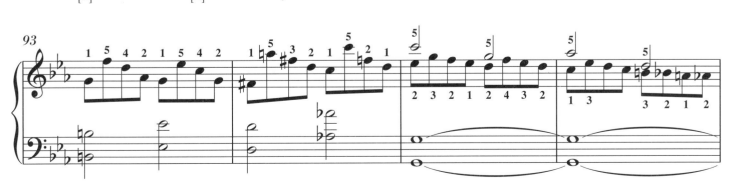

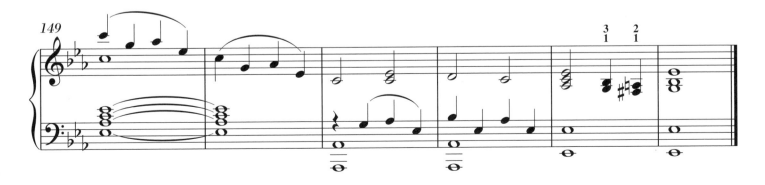

Starlight

Margaret Ruthven Lang
(1867–1972)

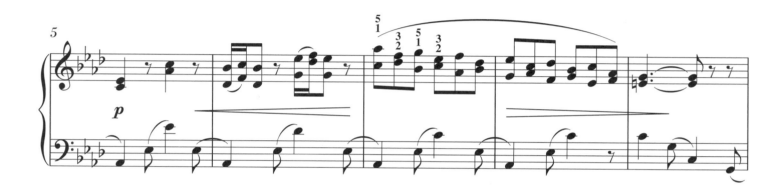

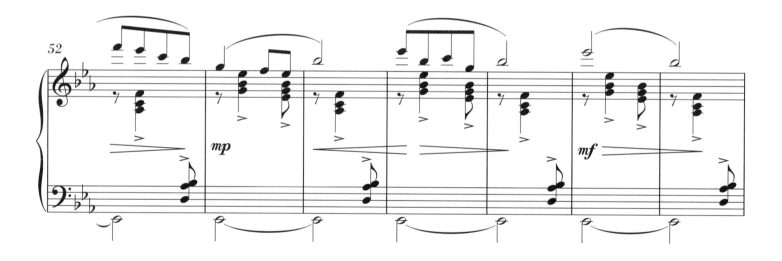

Tempo I

48

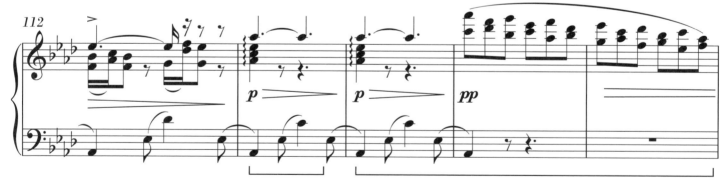

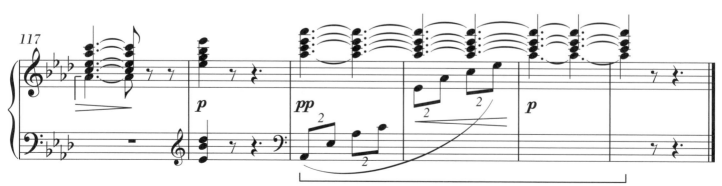

This page has been left blank
to facilitate page turns

Twilight

Margaret Ruthven Lang
(1867–1972)

Moderato (♩ = 100)

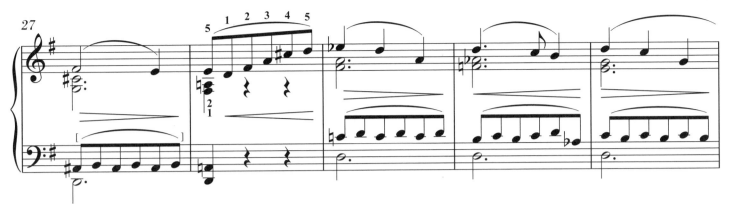

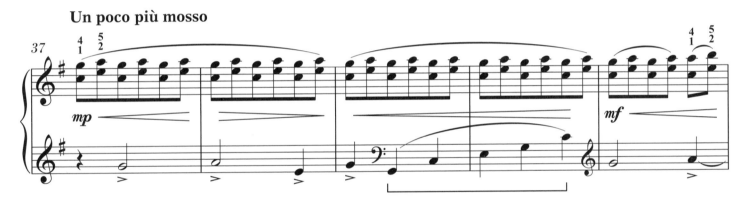

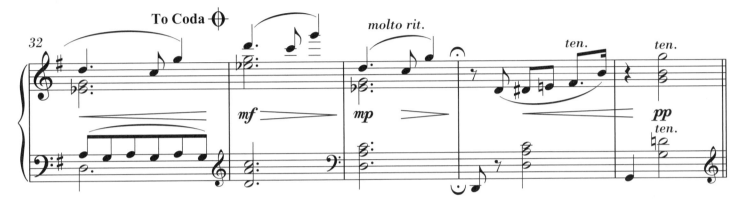

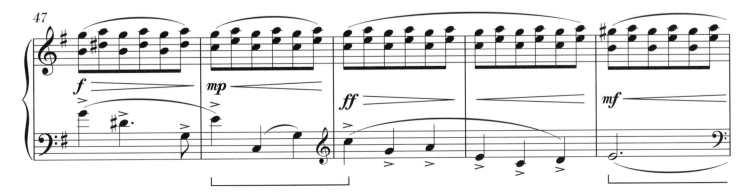

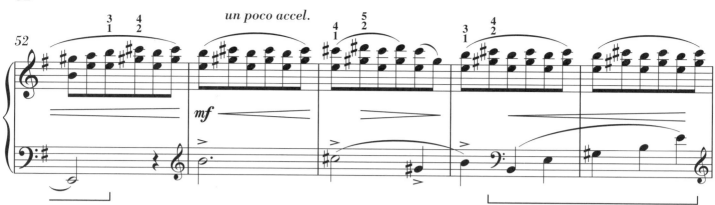

un poco accel.

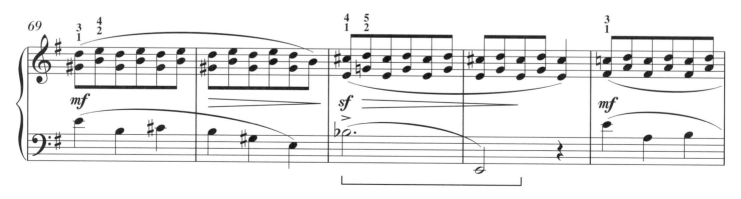

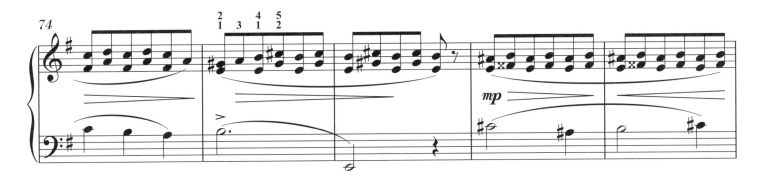

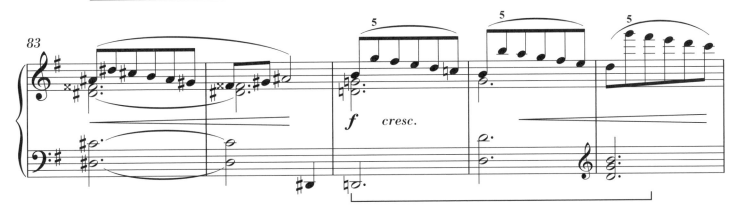

D.C. al Coda

CODA

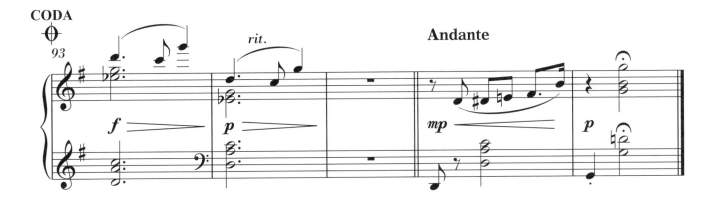

Andante

Staccato Polka

Clara Gottschalk Peterson
(1837–1910)

Con espressione

poco più lento

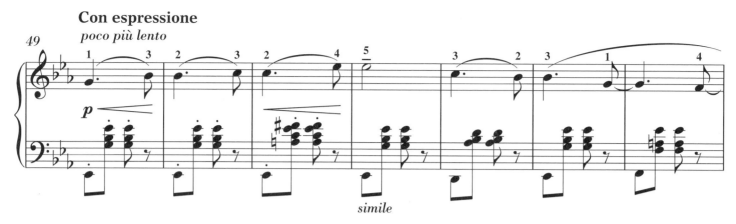

simile

lamentoso

Polonaise in C Major
from *Quatre Polonaises*, Op. 1, No. 2

Clara Schumann
(1819–1896)

Scherzo in G Major

Clara Schumann
(1819–1896)

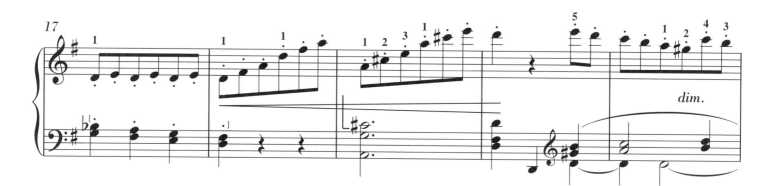

Trio
einfach

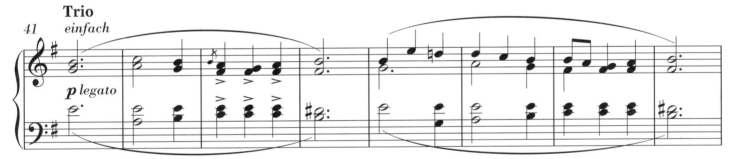

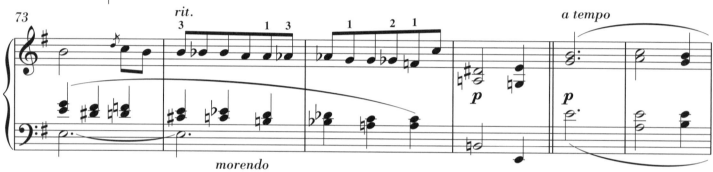

Tempo primo